ANTI-BULLYING BASICS

BULLIED *in Cyberspace*

WORLD BOOK

A Scott Fetzer company

Chicago

worldbook.com

Staff

World Book, Inc.
233 North Michigan Avenue
Suite 2000
Chicago, Illinois, 60601 U.S.A.

For information about other World Book publications, visit our website at **www.worldbook.com** or call **1-800-967-5325.**

The contents of this book were reviewed by Kari A. Sassu, Ph.D., NCSP, assistant professor, Counseling and School Psychology Department, and coordinator, School Psychology Program, Southern Connecticut State University, New Haven, Connecticut.

Product development: Arcturus Publishing Ltd
Writer: Anne Rooney
Editor and picture researcher: Nicola Barber
Designer: Ian Winton

Library of Congress Cataloging-in-Publication Data

Bullied in cyberspace.
   pages cm. -- (Anti-bullying basics)
  Includes index.
  Summary: "A discussion of bullying in cyberspace, including bullying by text messages, on social networking sites, and on webpages; discusses what causes bullying, how bullying affects bullies and their targets; contains advice and useful strategies for targets of bullies"-- Provided by publisher.
  ISBN 978-0-7166-2075-4
  1. Cyberbullying--Juvenile literature. 2. Bullying--Prevention--Juvenile literature. I. World Book, Inc.
  HV6773.15.C92B85 2014
  302.34'302854678--dc23
             2013024680

Anti-Bullying Basics   Set ISBN: 978-0-7166-2070-9
Printed in China by PrintWORKS Global Services, Shenzhen, Guangdong
1st printing November 2013

Contents

What Is Bullying?

Bullying is unwanted, deliberately hurtful behavior that is repeated over a period of time. Bullying is often about an imbalance of power—bullies may use their physical strength, popularity, or something they know about another person to harm or control others.

Forms of bullying

Bullying can take many forms, including verbal, physical, social, and cyberbullying (a form of bullying on digital devices).

- Verbal bullying includes name-calling, teasing, inappropriate comments, threats, and abusive comments.
- Physical bullying includes hitting, kicking, spitting, tripping, and stealing or damaging possessions.
- Social bullying includes deliberately excluding someone from social events, spreading rumors about a person, and embarrassing or humiliating someone.
- Cyberbullying includes harassment and abuse via a cell phone, on social media sites, or online.

What bullying is not

Bullying is not:
- single occurrences of rejection, nastiness, or spite
- random acts of aggression
- one-time arguments or disagreements

All of these events can cause unhappiness. While falling out with friends or dealing with occasional disagreements may not be pleasant, they are a normal part of the process of learning and growing up. These occasional "dramas" in everyday life are very different from bullying, which is deliberate and repeated aggressive behavior that is intended to cause harm and unhappiness.

ABOUT THESE BOOKS

This series of books—*Anti-Bullying Basics*—examines six different aspects of bullying: bullying by groups, bullying by boys, bullying by girls, bullying in cyberspace, bullying by friends, and bullying to "fit in." Each book examines the causes and effects of a particular type of bullying and provides support and practical advice for dealing with bullies. Bullying happens everywhere in society: It often goes unchecked because of the fear it creates and because people don't take it seriously.

Why it's serious

Bullying is serious because it can have a damaging effect on the person being bullied, on the person doing the bullying, and even on the bystanders who witness incidents of bullying. Bullying creates a climate of fear, and bystanders may be anxious that they will be next on the bully's list of targets. The targets, the people who are being bullied, are more likely to lack self-confidence, have low self-esteem, have difficulty concentrating, and suffer from depression and anxiety. People who bully are at greater risk than others of becoming involved in violence and crime. Bullies also have a higher risk of struggling or failing at their school studies. Young people who are both bullies and bullied are at the highest risk of mental health problems later in life. And, both bullies and their targets may have a more difficult time forming healthy relationships as adults.

What Is Bullying in Cyberspace?

Bullying in cyberspace, or cyberbullying, uses such communications technologies as cell phones and the Internet to bully others. It's just as unkind as other types of bullying. In fact, it can be even harder for targets to deal with because the bully can reach them anywhere, even at home. Nowhere feels safe.

> *"[Cyberbullying is] when the Internet, cell phones or other devices are used to send or post text or images intended to hurt or embarrass another person."*
>
> National Crime Prevention Council, Washington, D.C.

How it happens

Cyberbullying can take many forms—cyberbullies might send messages directly using a cell phone, an online messaging service, or e-mail. They might use social networking sites to post nasty messages or embarrassing photos or videos where friends can see them. Or they may make them public on such sites as Tumblr and YouTube. Some cyberbullies use online games as a route for attacks. Cyberbullies often use more than one form of communication. Unlike other forms of bullying, cyberbullying need not be repeated cruel behavior. Even one post online can take on a life of its own, as others repost and forward messages. The hurt caused by one comment can be magnified many times over. Occasionally, cyberbullying can be combined with other forms of bullying, such as physical or verbal bullying.

You are not on your own

Cyberbullying is very distressing, but if it happens to you, you don't need to suffer alone. There are many people and organizations you can turn to for help and things you can do to help the situation yourself. There is lots of information about dealing with cyberbullying in this book.

WHERE CYBERBULLYING HAPPENS

*Text messages – 16%

Websites – 23%

Chat rooms – 25%

E-mail – 25%

Instant messaging – 67%

(*Categories may overlap)

BULLYING Q & A

Is this bullying?

Q. Some of my sister's so-called friends post mean messages about her on Facebook. When she asks them to stop, they make fun of her and say she can't take a joke. But she doesn't think it's funny. Is she just being too sensitive, as they say?

....

A. If she is hurt by their actions and they will not stop, your sister should get help from a trusted adult. Encourage her to talk to her school counselor, school psychologist, or teacher about her problem. In addition, it is possible to unfriend people on Facebook and to report that a post on Facebook is abusive. See page 44 of this book for more information about privacy settings on Facebook.

Cyberbullying Is Different

Cyberbullying differs from other forms of bullying in some important and distressing ways. One big difference is that, unlike real-world bullies, cyberbullies don't necessarily have to confront the person they hurt.

Cyberbullying can reach a target at home.

A coward's way

Cyberbullying is a cowardly way of getting at someone because the bully doesn't have to see the target's reaction. The person being cyberbullied may not even know who is doing it. Distance and *anonymity* (having an unknown identity) can make the bullying even more hurtful than it would be if the bullies were present. From the cyberbully's point of view, bullying in cyberspace can seem less like bullying—it is often much easier to do shameful things if no one knows it's you doing them. It's also easier to persuade yourself that it's all just a joke if you don't have to witness the misery of the person on the receiving end.

Unseen harm

Cyberbullying doesn't produce visible wounds, but sometimes psychological damage can be as bad as physical injury, though there is no easy way of seeing the pain. Other people may not realize anything is wrong unless a target or bystander speaks out. It's easy to keep cyberbullying secret. If you hear of a friend who has been hurt by cyberbullying or learn that someone has engaged in cyberbullying, talk to an adult about what can be done to end it.

No escape

A target of real-world bullying often has some places where he or she feels safe. But a cyberbully can send text messages to someone asleep in their bed at home, out with their family, or even on vacation. They can reach targets in the evening through their computer. Cyberbullying can be both more private and more public than real-world bullying. Something posted online can be seen all around the world instantly and re-posted endlessly. It can be impossible to stop it spreading.

OVERCOMING SHAME

Morgan was ashamed that she was being cyberbullied—she felt it was weak to be so upset by what was happening and thought she was being too sensitive. Then one day she read an article in a magazine. It said that there is no shame in being bullied—it's the bully who should be ashamed. She hadn't looked at it that way before. She started to feel angry rather than ashamed. That anger gave her the courage to speak out and put a stop to what was happening.

Find the courage to speak out about cyberbullying.

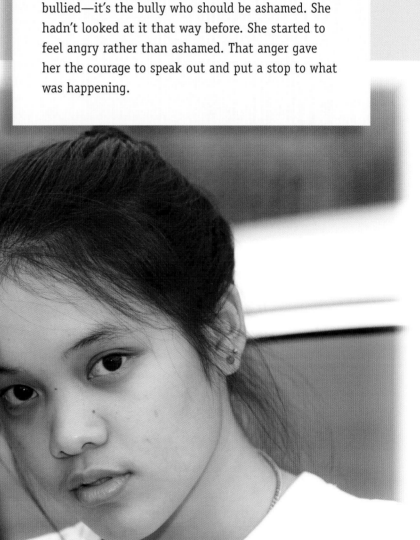

Instant Messaging

Online messaging is a great way of having fun and keeping in touch with friends. But it is also a very common place for abuse to occur. It's all too easy to send unkind messages using an instant messaging or chat service.

Online messaging is a great way to stay in touch with friends, but be very careful if you chat with strangers.

Take care

Instant messaging your friends—people you know in real life—is one thing. But if you accept chat invitations from strangers, you need to be extremely careful. Online friends might seem fine to start with but change their behavior later on. It's always dangerous to give out such personal details as your real-world location or cell phone number. If chat remains the only way someone can contact you, it's easier to avoid that person later if you need to. If someone turns out to be an online bully and knows a lot about you, he or she can be harder to avoid.

....

Cut them off

If someone is abusive, you don't need to keep chatting with him or her. Replying is a natural response, but this allows a bully to keep abusing you. A cyberbully will try to draw you into a conversation and keep you there, piling on more abuse while you try to work out what you've done wrong (usually nothing) or how you have provoked the attack (you probably haven't). Close the chat window immediately—and they can't get to you.

....

OTHER DANGERS OF ONLINE CHAT

When you "meet" people on the Internet, you do not really know who they are. You only know who they say they are. In 2007, a young woman thought she was answering an advertisement for a nanny position placed on Craigslist by a young mother. In reality, a man had posted the ad. He lured the woman to a house for a "job interview," where he killed her. A number of teens have been kidnapped and killed by adults claiming to be teens. NEVER give out personal information to strangers about who you are or where you live, and NEVER agree to travel to meet someone you know only from the Internet.

BULLYING Q & A

What's happened to my online friend?

Q. I made friends online with someone who knows my cousin. He was really nice at first. Then he started making mean remarks. I was upset and asked what I'd done wrong. Things quickly got worse; he's always putting me down and making me feel stupid. I don't have many real-world friends and I need him. How can I get things back to how they were?

....

A. It sounds as though this boy enjoys upsetting you and likely won't change back. Some people get a kick out of hurting someone else. Tell him that you enjoyed your early chats, but that you don't like the way he treats you now and don't want to talk to him anymore. You can and should block him so that he can't send you any more chat requests.

Texting

A cell phone can help you to feel safe when you're out and about, and it is great for keeping in touch with friends. But it can also be an effective tool for bullies.

24/7

Most cell phone bullying is by text message. The bully might send abusive texts or pictures many times a day, even disturbing the target's sleep. Most people look at a text message the moment it arrives. If it's an upsetting message, it can have an immediate impact.

Don't look now

If you recognize a bully's name or number on a message, you can avoid opening abusive messages. Sometimes, though, you can't see who sent the message, or you don't recognize the number. If you're being bullied, don't open messages from numbers you don't recognize. Although it's upsetting to receive abusive messages on your phone, don't delete them. They are the evidence you need to start fixing the problem. If you report the behavior, these messages can be shared with a school administrator or even the police.

Cell phones are useful for staying in touch with family and friends. But they also give bullies an easy way to reach you wherever you are.

Putting a stop to it

If the bully always uses the same phone number, you can report it to your phone-service provider. Your provider will either tell you how to block the number or do it for you. If the bully starts again from another number, or there are several bullies, you can ask for a new number for yourself. Only tell people you trust about your change of number.

CHANGE THE NUMBER

Andrea was getting horrible messages from a whole group of kids. It was really upsetting. Every time she looked at her phone there would be more. She always turned her phone off at night, and she got her brother to check her messages because she was afraid to. In the end, she got a new phone number and only gave the new number to her family and close friends. The bullying stopped.

ANTI·BULLYING· BASICS·

Never delete bullying text messages—you may need them as evidence later on.

Digital Pile-On

Being bullied by one person is bad enough, but being swamped by cyberbullies is very distressing. When a lot of people work together to abuse someone online, it's called a "digital pile-on."

All at once

Social networking sites are a good way to share photos, news, videos, and chat with friends. But they're also an easy way to send unkind comments and embarrassing photos or videos; such sites allow bullies to cooperate in abusive behavior. Digital pile-ons often involve a large number of people all posting cruel or mocking comments, sending unkind messages, or sharing photos and videos to humiliate someone.

All together

One or two people usually begin online abuse, but others can be quickly drawn into it. Many of the people involved in a digital pile-on might not think of themselves as cyberbullies—they are just joining in with something that someone else has started. Often, they take part without really thinking, acting in a spirit of excitement or fun, and without considering how the target of the abuse will feel. If you find yourself tempted to forward a message about someone or to re-post a message, think about how you would feel if this message were about you. Remember, forwarding or re-posting means you are engaging in bullying behavior, too.

Don't be tempted to join in with bullying behavior.

BULLYING Q & A

How can I deal with this bully?

Q. I fell out with a girl in my class and she started posting lies about me on my Facebook page. Soon, all her friends were doing it, too. They convinced new people to post about me when I deleted the original posters from my friends list. Then they started sending nasty messages in a chat window, so it was coming at me all the time. I don't want to go on Facebook anymore, but that's where I keep in touch with my real friends. What can I do?

....

A. As you discovered, you can delete posts on your own page and change your settings to prevent someone leaving more. You can also mark the messages as abusive. If someone keeps abusing you, you can report him or her to the social networking site. See page 44 for more information about how to alert Facebook about your problem. You should also contact someone at your school, such as a school counselor or trusted teacher, to report this problem.

Get out and have fun— don't live your entire life online.

Mean Talk

It's hurtful if someone says mean things to you directly by text or chat. But it can be even worse if mean, private, or false information is posted where lots of people can read it. The size of the audience increases the humiliation.

Cyberbullying can make the target feel humiliated and ashamed.

It's all about you

If someone posts abusive material on your social networking page, you can remove it. If they send you cruel text or chat messages, you're the only one to see them. But public bullying—when abusive material is shared with others—is distressing in a different way.

Cyberbullies might post on their own pages on a social networking site, on a micro-networking service such as Twitter, or on another website. They might deliberately place abusive material where the target will see it, or put it in lots of different places so that it's hard to control. All of this adds to the fear and insecurity that bullying fosters. According to a Cyberbullying Research Center survey of a group of 10- to 18-year-olds in the southern United States, the most common forms of cyberbullying are mean or hurtful comments (making up 13.7 percent of the abuse) and online rumors (at 12.9 percent). Other types of cyberbullying include posting embarrassing pictures taken of a target or making false accusations against a target online.

Fighting back

If you are being targeted by this type of cyberbullying, it's natural to want to defend yourself. However, it's best not to get drawn into an online argument or fight back with abuse of your own. It can make the problem worse, and you might even get into trouble for bullying yourself. Instead, keep screenshots of abuse so that you can demonstrate what is happening. If you find this too distressing, ask a trusted friend or family member to take screenshots for you. Some social networking sites have a button you press to report a post as abusive. Other sites allow you to block anyone you want through the privacy settings.

ANTI·BULLYING·BASICS·

Always keep a record of any online abuse and report it.

Spreading It Around

Sometimes, photos or videos can go viral very quickly, becoming immensely popular and gathering lots of views and re-postings. This can be devastating if you are the subject and you don't like the material. The speed with which harmful messages can reach lots of people adds to the trauma of cyberbullying.

Phone photos

Many cell phones can upload photos and videos immediately. You might be photographed or filmed doing something silly or embarrassing and then find that it's been posted to a social networking site or YouTube, or circulated on Twitter. YouTube, Twitter, and Facebook all have ways to block posts. If you are not certain how to block posts or delete posts about you, you can contact the sites.

It's easy to have a laugh about taking silly pictures, without thinking about whether they will be shared. Sometimes, photos are taken without the consent or even the knowledge of the person involved. And some cyberbullies create fake photos—putting someone's head on a different body, for instance.

Be careful about which photos you upload or post online.

Sexting

When you're happy in a relationship, you might send intimate messages or photos to your partner. Sending sexually explicit messages or images by cell phone is often called "sexting." If you split up later, those same messages and photos could be shared. It's always worth remembering that, however good your relationship is, it might not last. Do you trust your partner to keep very private things private? It's better not to create material that could upset or embarrass you later.

BULLYING Q & A

How do I get rid of these tags?

Q. I went out with some guys from school. One of them took photos and videos of me doing stupid things and tagged me in them on Facebook, then put them on YouTube and sent the link to just about everyone I know. I can't face going to school as everyone's seen the stuff. I just know they're laughing at me. What can I do?

....

A. If you're tagged in a photo or a post, you can remove the tag and it can't be re-tagged. You can ask Facebook or YouTube to remove really abusive material, but if it's just embarrassing, you might have to live with it. Although material spreads far and wide very quickly, it's also usually forgotten very quickly, too.

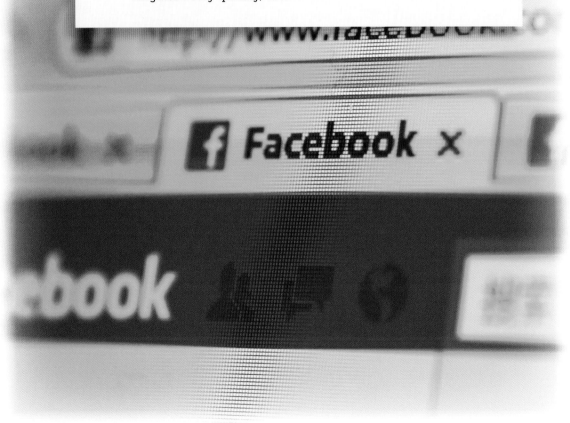

You can ask Facebook to
remove abusive material.

Drawing Others into Bullying

Often, cyberbullies draw others into online abuse. They might openly encourage people to join in, or they may just rely on the general sharing and social nature of the Internet to gather more abusers. Always take a moment to think before you re-post or forward any photo or message.

Polls and pages

Sometimes cyberbullies set up a web page, blog, or page on a social networking site specifically to abuse a target. Or they might use online tools to create a poll or image gallery as a form of abuse. Typically, a poll asks other users to rate how horrible the target is in some way, or rate their appearance, or vote on what horrible things they want to happen to them.

It's not fun

People who participate in this type of group abuse without themselves setting up the pages, galleries, or polls are still involved in bullying. If a cyberbully creates an online poll or page and no one votes or comments, it has no effect. Anyone who votes or comments on any of this abuse is behaving as a cyberbully.

If you "like" photos that upset or embarrass someone, or add mean comments, or vote in an abusive poll, you are just as guilty as the person who created or posted the material.

You don't have to be the one who posts abusive material to be a bully. "Liking" it or adding more abusive comments makes you a cyberbully, too.

SERIOUS THREATS

Aidan had been getting a lot of trouble from a couple of cyberbullies. When he blocked them from his phone and Facebook page, they looked for other ways to torment him. They used a survey page to create a poll. They asked people to vote on whether they should set fire to him, stab him, or tie bricks to him and throw him in the river. It was really scary. Because they made a threat to hurt him, Aidan went to the police, and they helped him to end the bullying.

Left Out

Being on your own is great if you've chosen it—but if you're on your own because no one wants to be with you, it can be hurtful and deeply upsetting. The same is true online. Being isolated or excluded online can be just as distressing as it is in the real world.

Bullying by doing nothing

Active cyberbullying includes people being deliberately rude, aggressive, and abusive—making cruel remarks or posting humiliating videos, for example. Passive bullying is bullying by not doing things. It includes people dropping someone as a contact or "friend," and refusing to engage with someone in chat, forums, online games, or social networking.

Excluding and isolating someone—which experts call *relational aggression*—can only be effective when a group of people act together. It relies on the bully drawing other people into the abusive behavior.

Isolated

Being excluded from social activities and gaming can make someone feel very isolated and alone. Sometimes, it can feel even worse than being openly abused because it makes the target feel they are not even worth being mean to. It is very damaging to the target's self-esteem and can lead to depression and self-harm.

Going online can be lonely if you are being cyberbullied.

EXCLUDED ONLINE

Ryan used to play online games with five or six guys. Then for some reason, one of them became angry with him. He started swearing at Ryan, but the game's moderator told him to stop. Then, he stopped playing online with Ryan, and he got the others to stop, too. Ryan was excluded from the group. That online game was something Ryan played most evenings, and it was hard not having it anymore. Eventually, Ryan found different people to game with. After all, life's too short to spend time with people like that, people who just turn on you and get a kick out of being cruel.

Being excluded online can be as hurtful as being deliberately left out in the real world.

Impersonation

Pretending to be the person you're bullying might sound like a strange thing to do, but it's quite common. The bully *impersonates* (pretends to be) a target in order to do things that damage the target's reputation. It can be very distressing and cause a lot of trouble.

It's a shock to find out that someone is posting material in your name.

Finding out

Sometimes, bullies set up accounts with social networking sites, chat, or e-mail services pretending to be their targets. Using these fake identities, they may make offensive posts or put up unpleasant photos and videos. It's a horrible shock to find out that someone is posting material in your name. Often, it will be quite clear to anyone who knows you that it's not really you posting. The information might present views very different from yours or might say something shaming and embarrassing that you would never post.

Real-world danger!

Sometimes a cyberbully may post a target's real-life name, address, or phone number online. This is very serious because it can lead to identity theft, or worse, dangerous confrontations in the real world. The target can ask for the false account to be closed down. He or she will need to prove their identity, and that the account has been created as a form of abuse. If the bully reveals personal details, the target can ask to have them removed from the site, but some damage may already have been done.

You won't be the only person to fall victim to an impersonation scam.

NOT IN MY NAME

The first time Grace realized that someone was sending hate messages in her name was when she had an angry e-mail from someone she knew only slightly. Once she realized what had happened, she had to e-mail everyone in her address book to let him or her know that if they got horrible messages that seemed to be from her, they weren't really from her account. She got a couple of messages back from people saying the same impersonation scam had happened to them. That was quite a relief.

ANTI·BULLYING·BASICS·

Hijacked

A common way of impersonating someone is to hijack his or her account. A cyberbully can only do this if they can access someone else's social networking or e-mail account.

It's not you

If someone gains access to your social networking account or e-mail account, they can do a lot of damage in your name. The most common way for this to happen is if you leave your account open on a computer while you are still logged in and another person discovers it and begins posting from your account. You can avoid it by always making sure you log out of your account when you're not using it. Don't let a public computer store your login details by using a "Remember me" setting, either.

Hijacked accounts

If a cyberbully does get into your account, he or she can shut you out by changing the password. The cyberbully can then control your account—posting abusive or embarrassing material or deleting your work or online friends. Most sites now send an e-mail if there is an attempt to change your password, which helps to prevent hijacking of accounts. But it's best not to use the same passwords for your e-mail and other accounts, just in case someone does discover one of them.

Be careful not to leave your account open; always log out when using computers in such public places as libraries.

BULLYING Q & A

How can I reclaim my Facebook account?

Q. I left a computer logged in to Facebook and my e-mail. The next kid who came along deleted some of my friends, changed my status—and then changed my password. He's carried on using my account, putting up hate messages and making me look like an idiot. What can I do?

....

A. You'll need to ask Facebook for help to reclaim your account. For the future, you might like to choose three trusted contacts. If you are locked out of your account again, they can help you get back in. Look on Facebook, under Security Settings, for instructions.

Protect your username and password from cyberbullies.

False Identities

As well as pretending to be the target, a cyberbully can pretend to be someone completely different. This is a long-term strategy that depends on building up trust with someone—and then betraying it.

Tina Meier wears a pin with a photo of her daughter, Megan, who hanged herself after being subjected to a campaign of cyberbullying.

Not who you think

The U.S. teenager Megan Meier hanged herself in 2006 after being duped into an online relationship with a boy who didn't exist. Megan was targeted by a group of adult cyberbullies after she ended a friendship with a daughter of one of the adults. They created a MySpace profile for a boy called Josh who befriended Megan. After a while, "Josh" turned against her, saying he no longer wanted to be her friend and that everyone hated her. The bullies said their intention was to make fun of Megan.

There's no one there

It's very easy for anyone to create a fake online profile. All that's needed is an e-mail address. If you build a relationship online with someone you don't know in the real world, it's important to remember that they might not be who they say they are. Giving out too many details about yourself can put you in physical danger, but even if you don't do that, you can still be emotionally vulnerable.

BULLYING Q & A

Who is this girl?

Q. I made friends online with a girl in a nearby town. She was really nice at first, but recently she's changed, saying I'm hopeless because I failed a paper, and criticizing my appearance in my photos. What have I done?

....

A. It's not what you've done, but what she's done. You don't know this girl in real life, so you can't be sure who she is. It sounds as though she's won your trust only so she can hurt you. The best thing to do is to put an end to the friendship and stop her hurting you more.

Just as this mask hides the wearer's identity in real life, many people hide behind fake identities online, too.

Who Is Bullied?

Anyone can be bullied and cyberbullying is no different. Anyone can be a target of cyberbullying—it affects boys and girls of most ages, and even adults.

How it starts

Cyberbullying can be triggered by an event in the real world, such as falling out with a friend. Or it might start with something online—you make a remark someone doesn't like. If you make a comment online that hurts someone or is misunderstood, it might be best to talk with the person you angered with a trusted adult present. This talk might help to put an end to the misunderstanding before it becomes a bigger issue online.

Of course, with some cyberbullying, as with bullying outside of the virtual world, sometimes there is no obvious trigger for bullying.

Cyberbullying affects people of all ages and sometimes there is no obvious trigger.

Very common

If you're cyberbullied, you certainly shouldn't feel alone. Various surveys have found that between 16 and 33 percent of U.S. high-school students have been cyberbullied.

NOT ALONE

Kelley was being cyberbullied, and one of the worst things was that she felt completely alone. She didn't know who the cyberbully was, but whoever it was obviously knew quite a lot about her, so she guessed it was one of her friends—maybe someone she saw every day. That made her scared to tell anyone in case she was talking to the bully! When at last she confided in a counselor at school, he told Kelley that he dealt with about a hundred reports each year of cyberbullying. That made her feel a little better.

It can be hard to trust your friends if you suspect one of them is a cyberbully.

Who Becomes a Bully?

Just as ordinary people from all backgrounds can be bullied, so ordinary people from all backgrounds can become bullies. Very often, bullies have been bullied or abused themselves at some time.

You don't have to start it

Bullies are not only those who start abusive behavior. People who take part in ongoing abuse by forwarding or re-posting abuse are also bullies.

....

Why bully someone?

When asked, people give all sorts of reasons for bullying. In 2009, a survey of young people who admitted to cyberbullying were asked why they did it. They were allowed to choose more than one reason:

- 58 percent did it to get back at someone
- 58 percent said their target deserved it
- 28 percent did it for "fun or entertainment"
- 21 percent did it to embarrass their target
- 14 percent did it to be mean
- 11 percent did it to show off to friends

By middle grades, more girls than boys are guilty of cyberbullying.

....

You are guilty of cyberbullying if you forward or re-post abusive material.

BULLYING THE TEACHER

Mr. Parry was a new, young teacher, and he wasn't very good at keeping control in the classroom. One of the pupils in his class started a fake social networking account in his name, and many students posted to it and made fun of him. The teacher found out and was really upset. The whole class got into a lot of trouble. It sounds stupid, but some of the people in the class didn't even realize you could bully a teacher! They didn't think of themselves as cyberbullies, and afterwards they felt really bad about it.

Effects of Cyberbullying

Cyberbullying can follow the target wherever he or she goes—at school, at home, on vacation. There is often no relief from the misery, and it can have serious psychological and physical effects.

Long-lasting effects

Being the target of cyberbullies is distressing and stressful. Never knowing when the cyberbullies may strike makes it impossible to relax. The constant worry can lead to anxiety and depression. Cyberbullying is twice as likely to cause psychological disorders as real-world bullying. If former friends become bullies, that can lead to distrusting others, social withdrawal, and loneliness. Avoiding school because of bullying can have lasting effects on learning and life prospects.

A study conducted over 20 years found that people bullied as children had higher levels of depression and anxiety in adulthood than people who had not been bullied. Those who had been both bullied and bullies had the highest levels of mental illness.

Cyberbullying can follow the target anywhere—even on vacation.

•••

Physical effects

The stress of being bullied can cause physical symptoms such as headaches, stomach upsets, sleep disorders, and panic attacks. Behaviors triggered by stress, such as eating disorders, self-harm, and substance abuse, also cause physical harm. Some young people have even taken their own lives because they believed there was no other way to escape cyberbullying. This is always a mistaken idea. Talking to a trusted adult—such as a parent, counselor, or teacher—is the beginning to fixing the problem of cyberbullying in your life.

•••

GETTING TO THE ROOT OF THE PROBLEM

May was the target of cyberbullying for nearly a year. In that time, she became withdrawn and depressed. She had anxiety attacks, during which her heart raced so fast she thought she might be having a heart attack, and she often felt sick and faint. Then she developed anorexia—an eating disorder in which people eat very little or nothing for psychological reasons. It wasn't because she wanted to be thin—it was because she wanted to have control over something. May couldn't control the bullying, so she controlled what she ate. Her rapid and dangerous weight loss alarmed her family, and they sent her to a doctor. When she went for treatment, May talked to her doctor about the cyberbullying. The doctor realized that the cyberbullying was at the root of her health problems, and that the issue needed addressing before she could begin to recover.

Cyberbullying can cause severe anxiety and, in some cases, lead to serious health problems.

Putting a Stop to It

Cyberbullying rarely stops overnight, so there are two aspects to tackling it. One is to get it to stop, and the other is finding a way to live with the situation while it is being resolved.

You can take control to stop online abuse.

Take control

There are some things you can do immediately to help protect yourself from further bullying.

- If you're being bullied by phone, contact your phone provider about changing your phone number. Once the number is changed, be careful about giving it out to people you do not know well.

- If you're being bullied on a social networking site, block or unfriend the bullies and report the abuse to the site.

- If you're being bullied on chat or an online game, block the bullies.

Control yourself

It's best not to respond to abuse. It might make you feel better momentarily, but it encourages the bullies to keep on abusing you because they find your reaction satisfying. Certainly don't retaliate. You could end up in trouble for cyberbullying yourself.

Get on with your life

It's hard to ignore any form of abuse, but your life is not lived entirely online. Do things with friends and family, play sports, help someone out with a task—lots of activities don't involve using the computer or phone. While you are doing other things, you're out of reach of the cyberbullies.

BULLYING Q & A

How can I take action?

Q. I'm being cyberbullied, but I don't know who the bullies are—so I can't block them. They send me text messages all the time but withhold their number. What can I do?

....

A. In the short term, check your phone less often and turn it off at night or when you're busy. Tell your phone service provider about the problem and see if they can change your phone number. If you can give examples of the texts, recording the date and time they come, this can help your provider track down the bully and take action against him or her.

Get involved in activities that take you away from your phone or computer.

Helping Yourself

There's a lot you can do to help yourself if you are being cyberbullied. Taking charge of the situation boosts your self-esteem and starts to resolve the situation.

You can do a lot to help yourself if you are being cyberbullied.

Feeling better about yourself

Being bullied can damage your self-esteem. It's important to remember that you should not be ashamed—you haven't done anything wrong.

Work out an action plan. This should involve working with an adult to log and store the abusive messages, which you might need as evidence. There are *apps* (applications) you can download to log bullying episodes.

Take charge

There are several things you can do to stop cyberbullies from contacting you.

If you can't stop phone bullying by blocking known numbers, ask your phone provider to give you a new number. Change your security settings on social networking sites so that your information is not public and is restricted to people you trust. Tell trusted friends that you don't like some of the material about you that you see online. They might not even be aware you are being bullied. Be brave and honest. Report all abuse to the site that is hosting it (such as Facebook, YouTube, or Tumblr). They might issue warnings to cyberbullies or even suspend their accounts.

TAKING CONTROL

Michael was being cyberbullied and it was getting him down. Finally, he decided not to let someone else choose how he felt about himself. He got angry instead of feeling frightened. He got a new number for his phone and changed the settings on his social networking page so that only people he really trusted could comment. Each time he was tagged in a photo or post, he checked it and removed the tag if he didn't like the content. When he changed his attitude, the cyberbullying soon stopped. It probably just wasn't satisfying to the bully anymore.

ANTI·BULLYING·BASICS

Changing your phone number and the settings on your social networking sites can end cyberbullying.

Sources for Help

You never need to deal with cyberbullying on your own. There are plenty of people ready to help you fix the problem.

Talk to a trusted adult—a teacher or a counselor, for example.

Speak out

The low self-esteem you may feel if you are being bullied makes it hard to speak out. But telling someone will help you feel better and deal with the problem. Only 10 to 20 percent of cyberbullied teens tell a parent. Many of them fear that parents will take away their computer or phone, which feels more like a punishment than help.

Teachers have experience and training in dealing with bullying, and your school should have an anti-bullying program. If the cyberbully attends the same school, the school might be able to intervene on your behalf. School counselors and psychologists can also help you to deal with bullies whether online or in the real world.

Expert help

Online support networks and helplines can also help, giving immediate emotional support at any time of the day or night. See pages 44 and 45 for some contact details.

If you are unwell because of cyberbullying, see a medical practitioner. Problems can get worse if left untreated.

The law

Laws about cyberbullying vary between countries and between states in the United States. Your school will be able to help you work with the legal system, if appropriate. Remember to keep evidence such as messages, photos, and screenshots, with dates and times.

BULLYING Q & A

How do I deal with Xbox bullying?

Q. A boy at school has been cyberbullying me on Xbox. He started being a bit aggressive in the game, and now it's become personal. But I see him at school and he never says anything. He doesn't even look at me.

....

A. Speak to a counselor or psychologist at your school. The school will have an anti-bullying policy and, even though the bullying isn't happening at school, they can probably help.

A student learns about courtroom proceedings while taking part in a mock trial involving a case of cyberbullying.

Is It Cyberbullying?

How do you know if you are being cyberbullied? There are other types of online abuse, too, which are dealt with in different ways. Use the checklist below if you are unsure about something that has happened to you.

Other online abuse

- Grooming involves an adult using online media to talk to and befriend a young person. This is usually done with the intention of meeting in the real world, often to develop a sexual relationship. It can lead to assault, abduction, or even murder. It's NEVER safe to set up a meeting with someone you have met only online—you have no idea who they really are.

- Cyberstalking involves obsessively following someone around cyberspace, looking at everything he or she posts and everything posted about him or her. Sometimes a cyberstalker is romantically obsessed with their target. There are other motivations, too, including envy and admiration.

- Controversial statements can prompt a personal attack rather than straightforward disagreement. This sort of abusive commenting is called trolling. Occasionally, trolls make threats of physical violence.

Stay safe online, and look out for any warning signs that you are being cyberbullied.

AM I BEING CYBERBULLIED?

Use this checklist of warning signs to help you decide.

- I have received mean or threatening e-mail messages, text messages, or instant messages.
- Someone has posted mean, hateful, or hurtful things about me online.
- Someone has forwarded my e-mails or text messages to another person without my permission.
- Someone has altered a picture of me online.
- Someone has taken pictures of me without my permission and posted them online.
- Someone has stolen my password and is sending messages or posting things and pretending to be me.
- Someone is excluding me from an online group.
- Someone has started an offensive blog or Facebook page about me or has started a nasty Twitter hashtag about me.

Additional Resources

Websites

http://www.anti-bullyingalliance.org/
A United Kingdom-based alliance of organizations that works to stop bullying and create safer environments.

http://www.bullying.org
A Canadian organization that provides educational programs and resources to individuals, families, educational institutions, and organizations.

http://www.bullypolice.org
A U.S. watchdog organization advocating for bullied children and reporting on state anti-bullying laws.

http://www.cdc.gov/bam/life/index.html
A Centers for Disease Control and Prevention (CDC) site for young adults about dealing with bullying, peer pressure, and stress.

http://www.thecoolspot.gov/pressures.asp
A site created by the U.S. National Institute on Alcohol Abuse and Alcoholism (NIAAA) for kids 11-13 years old.

https://www.facebook.com/safety/bullying
A campaign by Facebook and other sponsors asking everyone to show their support and spread the word against bullying. This page also has advice for people receiving abusive posts on Facebook.

http://www.itgetsbetter.org/
What began as a single YouTube video by author Dan Savage that encouraged young LGBT youth to tough it out through school, is now a website featuring thousands of videos made by youths and by celebrities attesting that life gets easier for LGBT people in adulthood.

http://www.ncpc.org/topics/bullying
A National Crime Prevention Council website, includes a page about girls and bullying.

http://www.nobully.com
An organization that helps schools to implement an anti-bullying program.

http://www.pacer.org/bullying/
PACER's National Bullying Prevention Center unites, engages, and educates communities nationwide to address bullying through creative, relevant, and interactive resources. PACER's bullying prevention resources are designed to benefit all students, including students with disabilities.

http://pbskids.org/itsmylife/
PBS advice site about issues that include family, friends, school, and emotions.

http://solutionsforbullying.com/Associations.html
Resources for parents, teachers, and other professionals listing organizations in different countries as a starting point for getting help.

http://www.stopbullying.gov/
A U.S. Department of Health & Human Services website with lots of information for kids, teens, parents, and educators.

http://www.violencepreventionworks.org/
A site for the Olweus Bullying Prevention Program, an American program that has been proven to reduce bullying in schools.

Books

How to Beat Physical Bullying (Beating Bullying series) by Alexandra Handon-Harding (Rosen Central, 2013)

Bullies, Cyberbullies and Frenemies (Teen Life Confidential series) by Michelle Elliott (Wayland, 2013)

Bullying (Teen Issues series) by Lori Hile (Heinemann 2012)

Bullying Under Attack: True Stories Written by Teen Victims, Bullies & Bystanders by Stephanie Meyer, John Meyer, Emily Sperber and Heather Alexander (Health Communications, Inc., 2013)

The Bullying Workbook for Teens: Activities to Help You Deal with Social Aggression and Cyberbullying by Raychelle Cassada Lohmann and Julia V. Taylor (New Harbinger Publications, 2013)

Confessions of a Former Bully by Trudy Ludwig (Tricycle Press, 2010)

The Courage to Be Yourself: True Stories by Teens About Cliques, Conflicts, and Overcoming Peer Pressure edited by Al Desetta and Educators for Social Responsibility (Free Spirit Publishing, 2005)

The Drama Years: Real Girls Talk About Surviving Middle School – Bullies, Brands, Body Image, and More by Haley Kilpatrick and Whitney Joiner (Free Press, 2012)

Friendship Troubles (A Smart Girl's Guide series) by Patti Kelley Criswell (American Girl Publishing, revised edition, 2013)

A Guys' Guide to Conflict/A Girls' Guide to Conflict (Flip-It-Over Guides to Teen Emotions) by Jim Gallagher and Dorothy Kavanaugh (Enslow Publishers, 2008)

Hot Issues, Cool Choices: Facing Bullies, Peer Pressure, Popularity, and Put-downs by Sandra Mcleod Humphrey (Prometheus Books, 2007)

lol...OMG!: What Every Student Needs to Know About Online Reputation Management, Digital Citizenship, and Cyberbullying by Matt Ivester (Serra Knight Publishing, 2011)

Online Bullying (Teen Mental Health series) by Peter Ryan (Rosen 2012)

Peer Pressure (Issues that Concern You series) edited by Lorraine Savage (Greenhaven Press, 2009)

Peer Pressure (Tough Topics series) by Elizabeth Raum (Heinemann Library, 2008)

Physical Bullying (Take a Stand Against Bullying series) by Jennifer Rivkin (Crabtree Publishing, 2013)

Queen Bees and Wannabes by Rosalind Wiseman (Piatkus 2002; rev. edition, Three Rivers Press, 2009)

Teen Cyberbullying Investigated: Where Do Your Rights End and Consequences Begin? by Thomas A. Jacobs (Free Spirit Publishing, 2010)

Helplines (USA)

Boys Town National Hotline:
1-800-448-3000 (available to all children; toll-free)

Child-Help USA:
1-800-422-4453 (24-hour toll-free)

National Suicide Prevention Lifeline:
1-800-273-TALK (1-888-628-9454, for Spanish-speaking callers; 24-hour toll-free)

Glossary

anti-bullying policies an agreed upon set of rules or actions to stop bullying

birth order a person's age in relation to the ages of his or her siblings (for example, being the youngest or oldest child in a family); psychologists believe birth order has an effect on personality

bystander someone who watches an event but who does not intervene

cyberbullying using such information technologies as e-mail, cell phones, and instant messaging to send harmful messages

desensitized having become accustomed to hurtful behavior

direct aggression openly aggressive behavior, such as kicking, hitting, or name-calling

eating disorder an illness related to ideas and behaviors about food and body image

exclusion being deliberately left out

gay homosexual; feeling sexually attracted to a person of the same sex (gay is a term more commonly used for men than women)

gender group a set of people of the same sex

hazing initiation ceremonies that can often be dangerous and abusive in nature

homophobia a fear of, or prejudice against, people who are homosexuals

indirect aggression a kind of quiet and sneaky aggressive behavior; it could involve such actions as spreading rumors or blaming a target for something he or she did not do

isolation feeling apart from or unlike other people

lesbian a woman who is sexually attracted to women

LGBT initials that stand for lesbian, gay, bisexual, and transgender

peer pressure feeling that you should do, think, or say something because that's what others your age are doing

relational aggression a type of bullying in which the bully tries to harm the target by damaging the target's friendships or lowering the target's social status

sibling rivalry fighting, disagreements, and competition between siblings (brothers and/or sisters)

social status how popular a person is, usually defined by the people around them

transgender a person who does not identify with the gender assigned to them at birth; for example, someone born as a male child may grow up feeling female and wear clothing and take on behaviors associated with female children

Index

Acknowledgments

Cover photo: iStock Photos (MachineHeadz)
Back cover photo: Shutterstock (Rommel Canlas)

Alamy:
17 (NetPics), 20-21 (Golden Pixels LLC), 36 (PhotoAlto).

Corbis:
10 (Mina Chapman), 22 (HBSS), 28 (Mario Anzuoni/Reuters), 33 (Hero Images), 35 (Julian Winslow/ableimages), 39 (John Lund/Marc Romanelli/Blend Images), 40 (B. Boissonnet /BSIP), 41 (Bryan Patrick/ZUMA Press), 42 (Owen Franken).

Shutterstock:
4-5 (wrangler), 6 (Andrey Shadrin), 7, 8, 12, 24 and 25 (Monkey Business Images), 9 (worac_sp), 11 (faysal), 13 (littleny), 14 (Denis Kuvaev), 15 (Jacek Chabraszewski), 16 (Sylvie Bouchard), 18 (Christo), 19 (Pan Xunbin), 20 (Aleksandr Bryliaev), 23 (Christy Thompson), 26 (icyimage), 27 (foto76), 29 (Max Topchii), 30 (Ammentorp Photography), 31 (Len44ik), 32 (CREATISTA), 34 (Neirfy), 37 (prudkov), 38 (Goodluz), 43 (Annette Shaff).